Mickey's Rules for Leaders

Mickey Addison

Lead The Way Media

Kailua, Hawaii

Mickey's Rules for Leaders

Copyright © 2017 Mickey Addison

ISBN: 978-0-9960193-5-4

Published by: Lead the Way Media, Kailua, Hawaii

mickey@leadthewaymedia.com

This book is available through Lulu.com and via Mickey's website at mickeyaddison.com, and also in eBook format.

Contents

Forward

Many leaders come up with their own set of "rules" to live by and guide how they lead. Search the internet for "leadership rules" and you'll get a huge number of results. When I searched, I got 55,000 results—not including infographics!

So why another set of "rules"? It's been profitable for me to learn from other leaders, and as I've matured as a leader some of the rules I wrote myself when I was younger have "grown up" right along with me. This book is the culmination of more than 30 years of leadership experience in the Air Force, as well as the lessons I've learned from others.

"Mickey's Rules" first published in 2015 as an eBook, and now it's in print to make it more accessible to more people. Leaders constantly learn—and it's my hope that in this book the reader will find some nugget to make them a better leader.

Lead the way!

Mickey

Introduction

Leadership is solving problems. The day soldiers stop bringing you their problems is the day you have stopped leading them. They have either lost confidence that you can help or concluded you do not care. Either case is a failure of leadership.

-Colin Powell

For years, I kept General Colin Powell's "Rules" on a worn, typewritten sheet of paper somewhere on my desk. His Rules had been published in a news magazine article, and I thought they were fabulous, so I typed them up and added a few of my own to the bottom. Over the years, I developed my own "Rules" that gradually replaced "Colin Powell's Rules" even though that worn piece of paper still adorns my desk. It's a reminder to avoid getting to cocky about coming up with my own rules—they came from my experience, yes, but also from leaders I admire.

I found these rules to be very useful to me, and every time I've violated them (yes, I *am* human) I've regretted it. The eleven rules listed below are my guidelines for leadership. They speak to being an *authentic*, *engaged*, and *principled* leader. As you read my rules, I challenge you to consider how you'll adapt them to your own leadership style and write your own.

Mickey's Rules

Rule #1. Have a direction and know what it is. Go there.

Rule #2. Don't spook the herd. Emotional demonstrations are always counter-productive and stifle initiative.

Rule #3. Don't let "perfect" be the enemy of "good."

Rule #4. "Can't" never gets anything done. Keep it out of your vocabulary.

Rule #5. The first report is usually wrong. Be patient and ask questions.

Rule #6. Asking the right questions is usually better than knowing the right answers.

Rule #7. The other team is not the enemy. The enemy is the enemy; don't confuse the two.

Rule #8. Be curious. Ask "Why?" a lot. Keep asking until you understand.

Rule #9. Walk the horses. No one can go full throttle all the time.

Rule #10. Drink your water, eat your lunch, and make new friends.

Rule #11. Check your "moral azimuth" …if you're doing something that you wouldn't want posted on the Internet, it's probably illegal, immoral, or fattening.

Rule #1: Have a Direction. Go There.

People ask the difference between a leader and a boss. The leader leads, and the boss drives.

-Theodore Roosevelt

The first rule of leadership is for you to know where you're going. People look to leaders for inspiration and motivation, but above all, they look to leaders for direction. That's why it's so very important for leaders to have a direction and move out.

Few things are more frustrating than when the person in charge lacks a clear direction. People get bored and restless when they feel like they're merely biding their time rather than accomplishing something. That restlessness can manifest itself in several ways: everything from listless employees who perform poorly, to bored employees who use their time for mischief. Highly motivated employees will feel frustrated at being held back, and will soon move on to greener pastures.

Leaders should take the time to define in their own minds where they want to take the team. This means spending time thinking. Duh, right? It's very easy for a leader to get mired in the day to day, and forget to look at the horizon. There's lots of ways to do that strategic thinking: in the morning, in a journal, an off-site, or some other way. The point isn't the *method*, it's the time the leader puts into charting his course. The journey may be important, but a perpetual journey serves no one.

Once a leader has a destination in mind, he must put in the hard work to get his team there. Setting goals are meaningless if you as the leader are unwilling to lead your team there. Leadership is an *active* job: to do it right leaders must be engaged. Getting people and teams to their destinations requires leaders to monitor progress, and adjust along the way.

Be an active leader: have the end in mind, then lead your team there.

Rule #2: Don't Spook the Herd.

The secret to success is good leadership, and good leadership is all about making the lives of your team members or workers better.

-Tony Dungy

My second rule, "Don't Spook the Herd" was born of several lessons I learned personally. Back in my cadet days at Texas A&M, I learned the importance keeping my emotions in check as a leader when I took over as an Assistant Squad Leader in charge of training my own squad of "fish" (freshmen).

On the second or third day of our version of basic training (benignly called "Freshman Orientation Week"), one of my new freshman cadets had done something wrong. I'm embarrassed to admit it now, but I responded with an animated display complete with arm waving, jumping around, and hollering. An upperclassman called me aside and quietly asked me pointedly if I thought my display was effective. I paused for a moment, looked back down the hall where my new "fish" were still at attention, and looked at their faces. A couple were scared, but most of them had a blank look of resignation. They weren't impressed, and they weren't motivated. I turned back to my upperclassman and said, "I guess not. Sorry." He replied, "OK, now go lead them and make them Aggie cadets."

Even if you don't come across as angry, a leader still must maintain calm on the outside. People will sense your emotions and respond—or react—to them in surprising ways. When I was a brand-spanking-new lieutenant, I was leading a group of Engineer Airmen on a local training deployment about 30 miles from our base. As I was leading the convoy, talking on the radio and giving orders, the master sergeant who was with me leaned in and quietly told me, "Sir, you need to calm down." In my mind, I *was* calm, but I was not *projecting* calm. I learned then that it was important for me to be more aware of how I looked and sounded, not just how I felt. You have to know yourself, true, but you also need to be aware of how your inner feelings are perceived by others. That's probably why some of the best leaders I have ever known have mastered this skill!

I have seen plenty of leaders who ruled by fear, but by far the most effective leaders inspire people to be better rather than being afraid. Keep it calm and carry on.

Rule #3: Don't Let "Perfect" Be the Enemy of "Good"

I know of no single formula for success. But over the years I have observed that some attributes of leadership are universal and are often about finding ways of encouraging people to combine their efforts, their talents, their insights, their enthusiasm and their inspiration to work together.

-Queen Elizabeth II

One of the hardest things a leader had to do is hold back enthusiastic employees or teammates who are so focused on perfection that they keep working on a project well past when they should have stopped. Sometimes "good enough" really is good enough. On one hand, you *want* employees to work hard and strive for perfection, but on the other hand there's usually more than one task to accomplish.

Of course sometimes you really do have to be perfect. So what's the right balance?

The key here is to look at *time* the same way as any other resource. Like all resources, time is valuable because it is limited. In for-profit, non-profit, and governmental organizations alike time has a quantifiable cost. Unfortunately, not every person thinks of time as a cost vs. benefit transaction. Put another way, leaders should always be asking themselves: "what's the return on my investment?"

Suppose a task takes an employee 40 hours to get the desired product but it is not perfect. Say it is 90% of what we wanted, and it will take another 40 hours to make the product perfect. Is 90% good enough? Maybe. What will it cost if my product is not perfect? Is it as perfect as my customer needs it to be, but not quite, up to what I was not it to be? Then maybe the extra 40 hours of time spent is not worth the 10% improvement.

Or, maybe not. If I have a demanding customer, or the 10% imperfection is noticeable and will affect my reputation, or if 100% is necessary for life, safety, or health then the cost-benefit analysis demands I keep working until it's perfect, then those extra 40 hours are not only worth it, they're necessary.

In addition to managing *time* as a resource, the leader needs to manage *employee morale* as well. Morale, like time, is finite and like time we can spend it. Unlike time, morale can be replenished. A wise leader knows when to require perfection and when to let "good enough" really be good enough. Avoid making changes to an employee's work because of personal preference (do not change "happy" to "glad"). Do not require more work than is necessary to get the job done right, and do not sweat the small things.

Employees will appreciate the freedom, and will usually respond when we ask them for perfection when it matters. Leaders should only demand perfection when it is necessary and no other time. To do otherwise could mean wasting time and employee morale.

Rule #4: Can't' Never Gets Anything Done

If you think you can do a thing or think you can't do a thing, you're right.

-Henry Ford

My Dad taught me many great lessons as I was growing up, but among the best was this one: "Can't never gets anything done. Keep it out of your vocabulary." Actually, the *exact* words he used were, *"Can't never could do anything."*

You see, Dad always believed that if you try hard enough, work hard enough and never give up, you can succeed. Through his encouragement, I came to believe it, too.

Now neither my father nor I believe that *anything* is possible. Some things are plainly beyond reach because of limitations in talent, or opportunity, or for some other reason. But history is replete with stories of people who meet with disaster and defeat, but never gave up and ultimately achieved their goals.

Take the story of Thomas Edison. He failed making the light bulb over 100 times before he finally succeeded. His quote that he'd succeeded in finding over 100 ways not to build a light bulb is well known. But despite the cliché of "try, try, again" the fact remains that Edison truly believed that electric lights were not only possible, but *inevitable*. We owe him for a wholesale change in our way of life.

Consider the story of NFL quarterback Kurt Warner. Warner went undrafted in 1994, and then tried out for the Packers only to be cut before the season began. He went to work sacking groceries for minimum wage until the next year when he made an Arena football team and played several seasons in that league, and the European league, before he got a shot at the NFL. He went on to a successful NFL career, winning Super Bowl XXXIV and named league MVP for the 1999 season. Warner believed in himself, and worked hard to gain success.

I doubt if the word "can't" is even in his vocabulary.

Growing up, Dad made sure we learned the "never give up lesson", and it paid off time and time again.

In Little League, I never expected to make the "Majors" my first year in—but I sure did my second year. When I was relegated to the "Texas" league the second year in a row, I was disappointed. Dad would not let me give up, though. "Hang in there," he said, "just do your best and it will all work out." During my first week of practice, it was plain to me that I was much better than most of my teammates. I worked out with that team for about a week before I got "the call" from a Major-League coach! He told me about my new team, and that it was my *attitude* that had prompted him to call me up. Despite having a terrible tryout, despite being out of sight ·on my Texas league team, I was getting "the call" for my stick-to-it positive attitude.

Now, no one can promise success. Like most, I have had my share of failure, but it's my view that true success comes as much from now you handle adversity, as how you handle the win.

Rule #5: The First Report
Is Usually Wrong

Pessimists are usually right and optimists are usually wrong.

- Tom Friedman

In my military career, I have had the unique opportunity to watch news bring made, both in Washington and in the field, then watch that same event reported on TV. I've also met many journalists, and in my experience they're usually trying their best to honestly report on what they've seen. However, it's also been my experience that the "breaking news" first reports are often at best incomplete and at worst completely wrong. That condition of "the first report is usually wrong" is part of the human condition and is not confined to journalism.

The first reports are not usually wrong because the people reporting the news are *trying* to get it wrong. The first reports are usually wrong because in fast moving situations it takes an enormous amount of skill and patience to sort the figurative wheat from chaff to find out what is really going on.

This condition is so prevalent that we spend a lot of time in military training learning how to sort through various facts and reports to discern the truth of a given situation. Everyone expects a little chaos in an emergency, so commanders and first responders learn quickly how to sort "possible" from "probable" and "true" from "false."

Those same "sorting" skills are useful in any situation when leaders have time-sensitive decisions to make and the information is coming at them in rapid bursts. Perhaps the hardest thing to do in a scenario like that is to breathe deeply and patiently ask enough questions to determine the veracity of the report.

The reason it is hard for leaders to be patient is that there is pressure to *act now* in a crisis. No matter if it is a terrorist attack or someone forgot to notify the customer their order is messed up, subordinates and teammates will look to the leader and demand *action*. What's more, leaders often pressure themselves to act, sometimes painting themselves into a corner where action is both inevitable and unwise. Good leaders resist pressure to act until the time is right for action. Somewhat counter intuitively, sometimes the best decision is *not* to act. Act or not, the leader has people looking at him wanting to know *what is next*.

Now, before I go on, there are certainly many instances where some action now is better than the perfect action later. Combat or emergencies are times when it is important to act as soon as possible rather than waiting on perfect information. It does not mean that those quick actions are rash or uninformed, rather, the soldier and the first responder *train* to face uncertain and dangerous situations so they have made their "cold consideration" many times over before engaging the enemy or running into the burning building. However, these instances are not the point of Rule #5.

Rather, the purpose of Rule #5 is for those crisis situations where there is a little time to figure out what is true and what is not. In those situations, the skilled leader takes a deep breath and *thinks* before he acts or speaks. The skilled leader is *patient* while she sorts out where she needs to put her attention.

Last tip: be sure to separate your skepticism of the accuracy of the first report from the truthfulness of the person making the report. People are usually doing their best. That requires the leadership maturity to be patient enough to figure out when and how to act.

Rule #6: Asking the Right Questions Is Better Than Knowing the Answer

> *We thought that we had the answers, it was the questions we had wrong.*
>
> *- Bono*

There is an old saying in the Air Force that colonels rarely ask questions to which they do not already know the answer. I never really understood that saying until I became a colonel, then the light came on. Everyone wants to show the colonel how smart they are, and further, few senior people like to be told what to do; they really want the colonel to let them do their thing. The same is true of CEOs and their VPs in the private sector. The skills that got an executive to a senior position are not necessarily the skills that make that senior executive successful.

I have found it useful to coach a solution out of a subordinate in most cases than to merely direct a solution. In fact, many times I have regretted giving direction to a problem rather than asking questions because even though it was efficient in problem solving, I ended up wounding the pride of a subordinate leader unnecessarily. When I have used questions to lead a subordinate to a solution, even when I knew in advance, where we were probably heading, I have been more successful.

The thing is, by the time an officer rises to the rank of colonel, everyone expects that officer to be a *strategic* leader not a *tactical* one. That means it is far better to stimulate thought among subordinates than to direct the answer to a specific problem. It is easy for any senior leader to know the answers-- chances are most have seen it all--it is much more productive to help subordinates come to the right solution on their own.

At some point, we all get a layoff notice. We change jobs, we are transferred, and we retire. If we truly care about the organization we work for, and the people we lead, we'll make sure the people who replace us are ready for the job and worthy of the responsibility.

Rule # 7: The Other Team Is Not the Enemy

One man practicing sportsmanship is far better than a hundred teaching it.

-Knute Rockne

Rule #7 may seem like it only applies to war or possibly sports, but it applies to business and life as well. Conflict can arise when goals or methods between people or organizations differ. People being people, this difference of opinion can rapidly become a conflict that escalates beyond the scale of the actual problem, and a barrier both to individuals or groups getting what they want. What's more, conflict between organizations can be a huge emotional drain on both organizations that saps creativity and initiative.

Contrary to the popular myth of the hard charging "corporate warrior" who thrives under conflict, most people do not want or like it. Most of us would much rather have calm and happy places to work, A perpetual state of conflict takes effort to maintain, and it consumes resources that could be productively spent on furthering the organizational goals. Imagine the staff time it takes to fight an "ad war" between to rival companies? It used to be just a matter of coming up with sharp advertisements, but in the age of social media and online reviews managing a reputation against false or misleading information can overwhelm small companies quickly.

The trick is to maintain relations with competitors and peers in what the military calls "Phase 0" (a state of peace or at least peaceful competition). There will always be conflicting goals, but in general, even in the modern marketplace there is plenty of "pie" for everyone. Starting a "war" with "the other team" turns the "other" into an enemy, and that usually comes from seeing others as enemies rather than as potential partners. That is a reason it's a good idea for businesses and individuals to participate in professional and civic organizations. You never know when you are going to find a friend or teammate.

I touch on this idea in my book, ***Leading Leaders***:

As a young officer, I missed an opportunity because I did not recognize a teammate when I saw him. In the early 1990s, the Air Force had adopted Total Quality Management (TQM) as an overarching organizational philosophy. As a result, we began a series of "awareness" classes in TQM theory and practice at each level of command.

During an exercise in my weeklong introduction to TQM, we were put into a team and given the task to produce paper airplanes. We spent considerable time developing our internal processes and then called over the "supplier" (our instructor) to negotiate a price for our raw materials. The goal was to spend the least amount of money and

*produce the most paper airplanes.
We quickly developed an adversarial
relationship with our "supplier,"
who repeatedly stressed that he had
plenty of "Grade A" paper for our
airplanes. After extracting the best
possible deal from our supplier, a
deal he assured us he was losing
money on, we produced a number of
paper airplanes. It was only after the
exercise was complete that our
"supplier" asked us why we did not
ask him about the rest of his product
line. "Why would we want anything
other than 'Grade A' paper for our
airplanes?" we asked. Then he
showed us the "Grade B" paper:
sheets of paper already folded in
half, and he would have sold them to
us at half price. That would have
saved a lot of work! Then he showed
us the "Grade C" paper: already
completed paper airplanes. These
were the least expensive of all, a
third of the cost of "Grade A" paper.
We had never asked our "supplier"
what else he had, nor had we invited*

him into our team. We had simply treated him as a resource to be exploited.

A teamwork approach could have gotten our little paper airplane manufacturing company a "win" against our real competitors (the other manufacturing teams) and saved us both time and money. Lesson learned!

Of course, not everyone is willing to "keep the peace," and sometimes conflict arises. Even in times when you are seriously hurt, it is useful to refrain from thinking in terms of unconditional warfare. In all but the most extreme circumstances, little is gained by crushing the opposition. In business especially, you are likely to have to deal with that person/organization again. It is best to avoid turning a temporary opponent into a permanent enemy if possible. However, when your livelihood or reputation is at stake and the other side is attacking ruthlessly, you must defend yourself. Be judicious in the application of power, crushing the opposition utterly will usually only extend the conflict. If you are magnanimous in victory, and gracious in defeat, it will open the door to detente and perhaps even future cooperation.

Soldiers understand this principle. It is only the most fanatical and committed enemy that must be annihilated. Usually it is enough to defeat the enemy and let them retire from the field with some dignity. America's World War and Cold War foes are friends and two of them are allies because the US extended the hand of friendship after the war.

Keeping the peace, both within and without, ensures our organizational and personal resources are spent furthering our goals, and not parrying the thrusts of a competitor.

Rule #8: Be Curious; Ask 'Why?' A Lot. Keep Asking Until You Understand"

Be less curious about people and more curious about ideas.

-Marie Curie

Successful leaders are curious about their business and the people who work for/with them. This sort of curiosity is an imperative for a leader because he/she must *both* accomplish the task at hand and the "care/feeding" of the team. To put it more succinctly, the leader needs to know what is going on.

There is a scene in the movie *Galaxy Quest* (DreamWorks, 1999) that is illustrative of this principle. When alien general Sarris (Robin Tobin) interrogates the human starship captain/actor, Commander Peter Taggart/Jason Nesmith (Tim Allen), he asks Commander Taggart/Nesmith repeatedly about the workings of an artifact on board the ship, and is incredulous when "the commander" says he does not know. You see, as an experienced leader, Sarris expects a commander to know his ship intimately.

None of us is very likely to be matching wits with an alien general, but the point for us is that the "commander" needs to understand how the organization works down to the "rivets and bolts." This means understanding who does what to whom, the stakeholders, customers, and teammates who produce whatever it is the organization produces.

The leader does this for a couple of reasons. First, it's not possible to diagnose problems if the leader doesn't know how the process works. Without that sort of detailed knowledge, it might not even be possible to know if there is even a problem! There's certainly not much hope for making process improvements. Second, it is much harder to look after the people if the leader did not understand the details of the organization and process. A curious leader who knows their people will know when there is something amiss with an employee. They'll notice when production drops off before it becomes a crisis.

There are some barriers to a curious leader, however.

The first barrier is the "this is how we've always done it" mentality. This mentality positively *breeds* a lack curiosity. Everyone is comfortable, no one attempts to improve things, no one notices inefficiency or wasted effort. "This is how we've sideways done it" is a recipe for organizational extinction.

The second barrier pertains mostly to senior executives and occurs when the staff and direct reports protect the executive from bad news. If the executive is not sufficiently curious to seek out bad news, or to go and see the operation personally, he/she can be blindsided with *catastrophic* news. As the saying goes, "bad news doesn't get better with age."

Perhaps the best reason for a leader to be curious is the effect it has on the team. If the leader is curious and engaged, asking "why" a lot, that behavior will become ingrained in the organizational culture. A climate like that will generate engaged employees, it will foster a culture of continuous improvement, and it will create an environment that improves everyone's job satisfaction. "Curiosity" is one of the best ways to ensure organizational success.

Rule #9: Walk the Horses

A good rider can hear his horse speak to him. A great rider can hear his horse whisper.

-Author Unknown

The 1949 John Ford film *She Wore a Yellow Ribbon* (Argosy Pictures) contains many lessons in leadership, and one scene pertains directly to Rule #9. You guessed it: they were walking their horses. What does "walking horses" have to do with leadership? Just this: leaders can and must try to get the best out of their people, but no one can go at a gallop all the time. The savvy leader needs to know when to gallop, when to trot, and when to get off and walk.

Back when I first joined the Air Force, leaders extolled the virtue of working the long hours. The guy who was at work the longest was considered the "workhorse" and admired for his dedication. We all bragged about how little sleep we got and how poorly we ate. No matter how dedicated a person is, they cannot maintain a breakneck pace forever. Lack of sleep, long hours, and bad food are a recipe for burnout rather than achievement. Thankfully, the culture has changed a bit and today's leaders understand the benefits of managing the workload.

That is where the *Yellow Ribbon* hero, Captain Nathan Brittles United States Cavalry (John Wayne), comes in. It was standard procedure on long patrols for the cavalry to get off and walk the horses a bit. It allowed the troopers to stretch their legs a bit, and gave the horses a break by taking 200 pounds off their backs. Having enough energy left in the tank (so to speak) meant that when the troop needed to hop on and gallop, horses and riders were ready. If the horses run too far or too long, they will be too exhausted when it comes time to sprint to the rescue of the wagon train.

The experienced leader works with the team to develop a "battle rhythm", a normal pace of business. Every business process/operation has a natural ebb and flow, with periods of "surge" where there's maximum effort ("gallop") and periods with much less demand on their personal/organizational resources. One officer I worked with went so far as to map out a 90-day period and code days as "red" (high tempo), "green" (medium/normal tempo), and "blue" (slow tempo) so he could plan ahead for things like employees' vacation planning and training schedules. As an executive, I have made it a practice to look for opportunities to encourage employees when to plan their leave/vacation, and when I had to plan for everyone to be working long hours.

Part of good strategic planning is developing and tracking the pace of operations. Make time in that plan to walk the horses.

Rule #10: Drink Your Water, Eat Your Lunch, and Make New Friends

Happiness is not a matter of intensity but of balance, order, rhythm and harmony.

-Thomas Merton

When my son was very young, he would give me the same advice as I left for work every day: "Goodbye, Daddy, have a good day at work. Be sure to drink your water, eat your lunch, and make new friends."

MIND BODY

SPIRIT

I always thought his farewell each day was far more insightful than just a small boy's simple advice. In fact, it is a great chance to talk about life balance.

There are many ways to understand and dissect the topic of life balance. My model consists of three focus areas: *Body, Mind,* and *Spirit*. The US Air Force has an outstanding approach to balancing the demands of work and life in their *Comprehensive Airman Fitness Model* that takes the familiar *Mental, Physical,* and *Spiritual* dimensions and adds a fourth, *Social*. And of course, there's always the familiar Maslow's Hierarchy of Needs.

No matter how you slice up the dimensions of the human person, the take away is that humans *are* multi-dimensional, and therefore leaders should be intentional about engaging the whole person and not just the external part. Each person has a body, mind, and the intangible part of themselves religious people call a soul, and everyone refers to as the human spirit. The point is that every person is more than meets the eye.

Being a leader means trying to find what motivates people, and what fulfills them, then intentionally working to harmonize those very personal needs with the needs of the organization. It's more than a mere transaction: leaders must recognize that their team is more than their collective job titles. They are people with needs and aspirations of their own, persons who have come together to do a job for their own reasons that may or may not be because they're drawing a paycheck.

The companies consistently rated best to work for seem to get that idea. They provide benefits that let the employees know they're valued beyond their contribution, but also valued as persons too. In each case the employees at those top-rated companies like their work and their environment first; the benefits are simply the externals. The companies that treat their employees as whole persons, with more than a single dimension, are the ones who get the most engaged employees at work in return.

So, the next time you look out over your team, stop for a minute and remember the words of my then four year old son: drink your water, eat your lunch, and make new friends. Living life balance as a leader is challenging. There are a lot of demands on a person's time when they're in charge, but finding time to feed all aspects of your body and soul is a key to any successful life. Anyone can put their head down and power through life; it takes a mature leader to understand that how you live is equally important to what you accomplish.

Rule #11: Check Your Moral Azimuth

az·i·muth [az-uh-muhth] noun

1. Astronomy, Navigation, the arc of the horizon measured clockwise from the south point, in astronomy, or from the north point, in navigation, to the point where a vertical circle through a given heavenly body intersects the horizon.

2. Surveying, Gunnery. the angle of horizontal deviation, measured clockwise, of a bearing from a standard direction, as from north or south.

It seems a constant to me that people who get themselves into trouble with their families, their workplace, or the law are usually caught living a hidden or double life. Whether it's the website a husband doesn't want his wife to know about or the businesswoman fudging on her company expense account, people hide what they know is illicit. We see it all the time in the news: politicians caught doing the very thing they campaigned against, military leaders violating their code of conduct, and seemingly average people living secrets that when exposed resulted in arrest and sometimes horrible crimes. The interesting thing is on the whole people *know* when they're doing something wrong. If we're doing something that we wouldn't want posted on the company bulletin board, it's not likely healthy behavior. As my mother used to say, "It's either illegal, immoral, or fattening."

President Ronald Reagan once said that character does not just "happen" at times of crisis; it is constructed bit by bit by seemingly insignificant decisions. Our character is the compass on which we guide our decisions and our lives. When we must make decisions, particularly those that involve morals, money, or the mission, we consult our character compass. I call it "checking your moral azimuth"

Of course, a compass is of no value unless it points north. So it is with our internal compass. As I have written before, to be useful a compass cannot be self-referencing. For those of us in the military, that external orientation is our Core Values and our Oath. For others, the "North Star" is their religious beliefs or political philosophy, or perhaps their professional code of ethics like the ones for physicians or engineers. For companies large and small, that orientation should include personal ethics and the organizational mission. When leading a team, leaders must foster a shared vision and shared code of ethics, because no team can be successful when traveling in multiple directions at once. Not everyone has to pray or vote the same way, but everyone should buy into the same organizational values and goals.

Living a hidden or double life usually means eventual personal and professional disaster. It was true 30 years ago, and in the internet age it's even more true that secrets do not stay secret for long. In other words, successful people live an integrated life free from hidden activities. They are the same person on Monday morning they were Saturday night. This sort of consistent approach is a recipe for excellence.

Excellence is not only the standard of what we seek to achieve, it is the expectation of those we serve as leaders. We also have the right to expect mission success and high personal standards from each other.

Finally, we must be on a good azimuth, the right "compass heading," when making decisions about our jobs or our lives. Having the right direction is important for any person, but it's crucial for leaders because people *will* follow us and do what we do. From making decisions on personal finances, to personal risk management, to the discipline to follow that same checklist for the umpteenth time, staying on the correct moral azimuth will ensure we make the right decision.

As much as we try to set a good example, no one can make decisions for another person. Each person must have a mature enough sense of personal responsibility to make good decisions for himself. It is the leader's responsibility to set and maintain a culture of excellence and responsibility, but ultimately we make our own choices.

Whether it's navigating the businesses landscape or making a low-level bomb run, checking your compass is an accepted part of our habit pattern. It's just as important to check our moral azimuth—and that's a skill for success in life.

Summary

In this book, I have showed you how to apply my Rules in your own life and business. These Rules have worked for me in every situation from small unit leadership to commanding thousands. I hope you found some application in your own leadership journey. The real take-away shouldn't be "go and copy Mickey." Rather, I encourage you to go and make these Rules your own in the same way I made General Powell's my own: by adapting them and eventually replacing them with *your* rules. In this way, you will become the leader you are meant to be, and can chart your own course.

Lead the Way!

About The Author

Mickey Addison, Colonel, USAF (ret), MSCE, PMP believes everyone can reach high levels of performance if inspired and led. During his 30 year US Air Force career, Mickey commanded thousands of Airmen, managed portfolios worth billions of dollars, and worked with military, civil, and industry officials around the world.

He holds a bachelor of science in Industrial Engineering from Texas A&M, and three masters degrees: Civil Engineering (UTSA) and Military Strategy (Air University), and National Strategy from the prestigious Eisenhower School in Washington DC where he was a

Distinguished Graduate. He is a certified Project Management Professional.

Mickey is the author of *Leading Leaders: Inspiring, Empowering, and Motivating Teams, Leading Leaders: The Workbook, Patio Wisdom,* and *The Five Be's.* He's a frequent contributor to industry publications and writes for his own Lead High Performance blog, People Development Magazine, and GeneralLeadership.com.

Other Books by Mickey

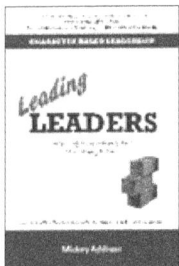

Leading Leaders: Inspiring, Empowering, and Motivating Teams

Leading Leaders is straightforward advice for leaders at all levels on how to be successful. Developed over a 26 year military career and a lifetime of leading, Colonel Mickey Addison lays out the foundation for character-based leadership. Illustrated through personal stories and anecdotes, Leading Leaders is a must-read for anyone who wants to improve their productivity and their character.

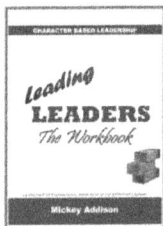

Leading Leaders: The Workbook

Leading Leaders: The Workbook is a companion to Mickey Addison's acclaimed work by the same title, but can be used as a stand-alone guide for discussion groups, seminars, and individual study.

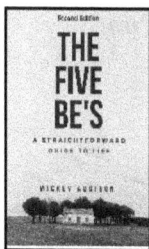

The Five Be's

In a world full of "no" and "don't", *The Five Be's* is a positive vision of who to "Be." Based on a lifetime of mentoring young adults, *The Five Be's* is a roadmap to living a healthy, fulfilling, and successful life!

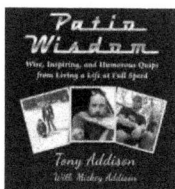

Patio Wisdom: Wise, Inspiring, and Humorous Quips from Living a Life at Full Speed

Inside are the musings from Living a Life at Full Speed, where wisdom comes from the School of Hard Knocks. It's wisdom born of adventure and hardship, joy and pain, victory and defeat—and everything in between. Illustrated with the author's own photos, and narrated with quips and memories, Patio Wisdom will leaving you in tears and stitches.

All of Mickey's books are available at

www.mickeyaddison.com

Book Mickey to speak at your event!

The Five Be's is by far Mickey's most requested talk, and he's delivered it to audiences from Middle School to seasoned executives.

Mickey speaks on of leadership and personal development. He's an engaging and inspiring speaker available for speaking engagements and workshops. Mickey will work with you to develop a program that suits your particular needs: personalized and relevant to your organization!

Mickey is available for:

- Keynotes/Presentations
- Workshops & Breakouts
- Team building events

Contact Mickey via email at Mickey@LeadHighPeformance.com to get started.